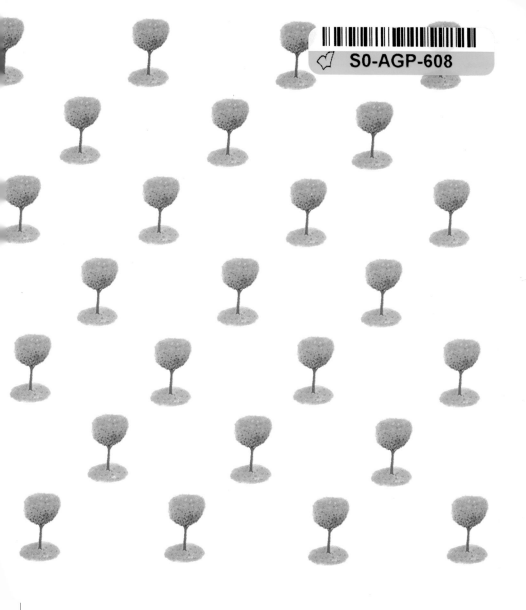

To

Our darling Rehan on
his 3rd Birthday

from

Aunty Pekka, Uncle Peter,
Kovalan Anna + Koleila Acca

U.K.

12 Aug '10

Happy is anyone who becomes wise – who gains understanding.

Wisdom can make your life pleasant and lead you safely through it. Those who become wise are happy; wisdom will give them life.

FROM PROVERBS 3

The Lord's Prayer
and Ten Commandments

Retold by Lois Rock
Illustrated by Debbie Lush

LION
CHILDREN'S

Contents

Aʙᴏᴜᴛ Tʜᴇ Lᴏʀᴅ's Pʀᴀʏᴇʀ

*T*he Lord's prayer was taught by a man named Jesus to his followers.

Two thousand years ago, this Jesus was born to a mother named Mary. His first cradle was a simple manger in a stable in Bethlehem. Yet ancient stories relate that an angel had told Mary that her child was the Son of God, and that angels sang in the skies above Bethlehem on the night that he was born.

When Jesus grew to be a man, he became much talked about in the villages around his home. Many claimed that he could work miracles, healing people with a touch. He was also a great storyteller, and crowds gathered to listen to him.

One story he told was about a father who had two sons. Together, they farmed the land to make their living.

The younger son had dreams of living a more exciting life on his own.

One day, he claimed his share of the family money and went to a distant land. There, he spent all he had on the glamorous things that money can buy.

Then famine struck. Soon, the young man had no money. He had to take a job minding a herd of pigs, and he was so hungry he wished he could eat the pigs' food.

Sad and dejected, he made the long journey home. 'Surely my father will hire me as a servant,' he thought to himself as he travelled along.

Then he heard running. His father had seen him coming, and was running to greet him. He took him home, welcomed him back as a beloved son and gave a joyful party in celebration.

'The God who made this world is like that father,' Jesus explained to his listeners.

He said that the God of the universe longs to welcome everyone with love and laughter and he told his followers how they could speak to God in prayer, as a child speaks to a parent whom they can love and trust.

Our Father, who art in heaven,

Are we alone in a vast, spinning universe... or does someone watch over us, as a parent watches over a child?

hallowed be thy Name.

And if there is a someone,
then that Someone must be

strong,

  life-giving,

      gentle,

          good

              and loving.

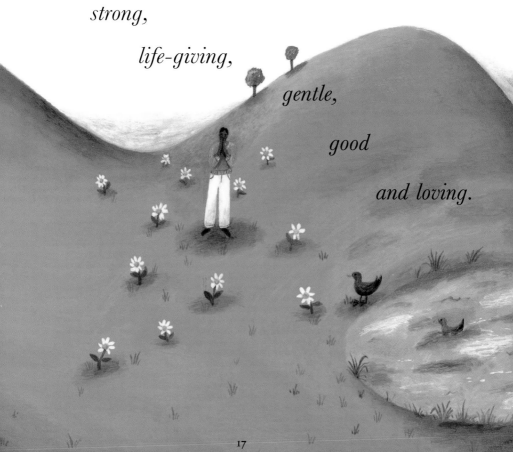

17

Thy kingdom come,

So may goodness
and love rule
in this world.

Thy will be done,
on Earth
as it is in Heaven.

May goodness and love rule
through all the universe, both
seen and unseen.

Give us this day our daily bread.

May the world's people have all they need to live in simplicity and joy.

And forgive us our trespasses,

*When we fail to be good
and loving,
may we be forgiven.*

as we forgive
those who
trespass
against us.

When we are wronged,
may we learn to forgive.

And lead us not into temptation,

May we never fall prey to hatred,
greed and wickedness.

but deliver us
from evil:

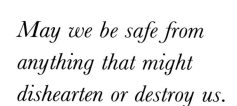

*May we be safe from
anything that might
dishearten or destroy us.*

For thine is the kingdom, the power
and the glory, for ever and ever. Amen.

About the Ten Commandments

*L*ong ago, as the Bible says, a man named Moses went to the top of a holy mountain named Sinai. There, on a rocky peak that rises above the barren land to the east of Egypt, God gave him the commandments that were to guide his people.

On the plain below, the people of Israel watched in fear. Thunder crashed, and a mighty trumpet blast echoed among the rocks. Lightning flashed down from the summit; smoke billowed around the mountainside.

Moses returned with a message from God: 'You have seen how I, the Lord, have spoken to you from heaven. Do not make for yourselves gods of silver or gold to be worshipped in addition to me.'

It was tempting to do so, nonetheless. The nations all around made images of wood, stone and metal, and worshipped them as gods. Some of these nations had grown powerful and wealthy. The Israelites were a refugee nation, on the run from the land of Egypt, where they had been slaves. So they did as other powerful nations had done and built a golden calf to worship.

Moses was stern in his response. He reminded his people that God had enabled them to escape, making for them a pathway through the sea. God had provided them with food and water in the wilderness. Now God was taking them to a land that they could make their home, and where they would be free to live as God's people. The laws told them how to worship God, and how to treat their fellow human beings

with justice, honesty and goodness. By keeping God's laws, they would enjoy the fullness of God's blessing in their new land.

'Israel, remember this! The Lord—and the Lord alone—is our God. Love the Lord your God with all your heart, with all your soul, and with all your strength. Never forget these commands that I am giving you today. Teach them to your children. Repeat them when you are at home and when you are away, when you are resting and when you are working.'

The commandments were written on tablets of stone and kept in a golden box in the innermost part of the nation's place of worship. They were recorded in the writings of the people and copied faithfully from scroll to scroll. They were handed down from generation to generation, and poets sang of the greatness of the law.

'Happy are those who find joy in obeying the law of the Lord.
They are like trees that grow beside a stream,
That bear fruit at the right time,
And whose leaves do not dry up.
The righteous are guided and protected by the Lord.'

The Ten Commandments are the great summary of all the laws. They belong to and are cherished by the descendants of the people of Israel, known today as the Jews, and they are honoured by Christians, who share the same heritage of stories. They are respected all over the world for the guidance they give in showing people a way to live that is good and right.

God spoke all these words, saying,

I am the Lord your God, who brought you out of the land of Egypt... You shall have no other gods but me.

If you would keep these commandments, then you must know that there is one God, one alone whom you must honour.

You shall not make
for yourself graven
images... you shall
not bow down to
them or serve them.

Beware of worshipping material things.
Do not put your trust in them.

You shall not take the name
of the Lord your God in vain.

Be careful when you speak of God.
Do not claim that you can speak
on God's behalf.

43

Remember the sabbath
day and keep it holy.

Enjoy the rhythm of the days:

six for work

and one for rest.

Honour your father
and your mother.

Give respect to those
who gave birth to you,
those who raised you.

You shall not kill.

God alone gives life,
and you do not have the
right to take it away.

You shall not
commit adultery.

God made man and
woman to live together
in faithfulness and love
all their lives.

You shall
not steal.

*Respect what
belongs to others...
it is theirs to enjoy.*

You shall not bear false witness against your neighbour.

Speak the truth of others; weave no lies.

You shall not covet anything
that is your neighbour's.

*Do not look greedily at what
others have. Only trust in God,
and do good.*

57

Happy are those who find joy in obeying
the Law of the Lord.

They are like trees that grow beside a
    stream,
that bear fruit at the right time,
and whose leaves do not dry up.

The righteous are guided and protected
by the Lord.

FROM PSALM 1

Text retold by Lois Rock
Illustrations copyright © 1999, 2000 Debbie Lush
This edition copyright © 2006 Lion Hudson

The moral rights of the author and illustrator
have been asserted.

A Lion Children's Book
an imprint of
Lion Hudson plc
Wilkinson House, Jordan Hill Road,
Oxford OX2 8DR, England
www.lionhudson.com
UK ISBN 978-0-7459-4941-3
USA ISBN 978-0-8254-6261-0

First edition 2006
3 5 7 9 10 8 6 4 2

Printed and bound in Singapore

Distributed by:
UK: Marston Book Services Ltd, PO Box 269, Abingdon, Oxon OX14 4YN
USA: Trafalgar Square Publishing, 814 N Franklin Street, Chicago, IL 60610
USA Christian Market: Kregel Publications, PO Box 2607, Grand Rapids, MI 49501

Acknowledgments

Bible extracts (introduction to The Ten Commandments) from
Exodus 20:22–23, Deuteronomy 6:4–7, Psalm 1 (adapted).
The Ten Commandments adapted from Exodus 20:1–17,
Deuteronomy 5:7–21. Scriptures quoted from the Good News
Bible published by The Bible Societies/HarperCollins
Publishers Ltd, UK © American Bible Society 1966, 1971,
1976, 1992, used with permission.
A catalogue record for this book is available
from the British Library

Typeset in 18/24 Baskerville MT Schoolbook and
20/24 Calligraphic 421 BT

Printed and bound in Singapore

Distributed by:
UK: Marston Book Services Ltd, PO Box 269, Abingdon,
Oxford, OX14 4YN
USA: Trafalgar Square Publishing, 814 N. Franklin Street,
Chicago, IL 60610
USA Christian Market: Kregel Publications, PO Box 2607,
Grand Rapids, Michigan 49501